mel bay presents

christmas solos for beginning cello

level 1

by craig duncan

PIANO ACCOMPANIMENT

D0871062

1 2 3 4 5 6 7 8 9 0

Contents

These arrangements have been designed to be enjoyed in a number of settings. There are companion books for violin and viola. Each book has the melody and a harmony part, along with piano accompaniment. Suggested uses are:

1. Solo cello with piano accompaniment.

2. Cello duets.

3. Cello and violin duets and trios with the violin book.

4. Cello and viola duets and trios with the viola book.

5. String ensemble using the melody and harmony parts in the violin book, and the harmony parts in the viola and cello books. The cello book can also be played by a bass.

Joy to the World

George Frederick Handel

The First Nowell

English Carol

Angels We Have Heard on High

French Carol

Good King Wenceslas

Traditional Carol

Ding, Dong, Merrily on High

English Carol

The Rocking Carol

English Carol

Once in Royal David's City

English Carol

Silent Night

Franz Gruber 1818

While Shepherds Watched Their Flocks

Traditional

* The beginning cellist may prefer to play the bottom note in measures 5 and 8 to avoid shifting.

Away in a Manger

Two Traditional Melodies

Jingle Bells

J. Pierpont

O Come, All Ye Faithful

Adeste Fideles

John Francis Wade, 1743

Deck the Halls

English Carol

The Holly and the Ivy

English Carol

Here We Come A-Wassailing

English Carol

We Wish You a Merry Christmas

Traditional Carol